Four Seasons *of* Verse

Four Seasons *of* Verse

The Right Words *at the* Right Times

Marcellus C. Miller

© 2010 by Marcellus Miller. All rights reserved.
2nd Printing 2014

Trusted Books is an imprint of Deep River Books. The views expressed or implied in this work are those of the author. To learn more about Deep River Books, go online to www.DeepRiverBooks.com.

No part of this publication may be reproduced, stored in a retrieval system, or transmitted in any way by any means—electronic, mechanical, photocopy, recording, or otherwise—without the prior permission of the copyright holder, except as provided by USA copyright law.

All Scripture quotations unless otherwise indicated are taken from the *King James Version* of the Bible.

Scripture quotations marked AB are taken from the *Amplified Bible, Old Testament*, © 1965 and 1987 by The Zondervan Corporation, and from *The Amplified New Testament*, © 1954, 1958, 1987 by The Lockman Foundation. Used by permission.

Scripture quotations marked TNIV are taken from the *Holy Bible, Today's New International Version®. TNIV®*. Copyright© 2001, 2005 by Biblica, Inc.™ Used by permission of Zondervan. All rights reserved worldwide. www.zondervan.com

ISBN 13: 978-1-63269-085-2
Library of Congress Catalog Card Number: 2010907969

Dedication

This work is dedicated to the many people in my life who have inspired, nurtured, supported me, and even those who tried to stand in the way of this gift. Without the opposition, I might not have been fully able to enjoy the feeling of overcoming the obstacles in my way. There are too many people who are behind me to name for fear of leaving one out. I know that you all know who you are and I love you all. However, I do want to extend special thanks to my immediate family, George Miller, Sr. (Pops), Janice Miller (Mom), Sheila Johnson (sister), and George Miller, Jr. (brother/best friend). You all know that I am nothing without the encouragement you constantly and willingly give. I owe you all my life.

In addition, I would like to thank Apostle Dr. Lonnie Brown, who indirectly inspired me to continue to look at words in a different light. I have to give all honor and praise due to God the Father, Son, and Holy Spirit. I truly would not be here if it were not for Him in my life. There are many who say that, but few who really understand it; I am in that few. I have written this work to offer my gift back to Him through helping others deal with different phases in their lives. He is the source of my life as well as the author and finisher of my faith. I am incomplete and desolate without Him so I want to thank Him for being in my life. He deserves all the praise, honor, and glory due His name.

This work is the culmination of many years of diligence and service to God, my family, my friends, and those in need. I trust that the reader sees more than mere words, but rather images of life's stories streaming by.

Contents

Prologue xi

SEASON I: SPRING
Spring Defined 1
Ghetto Child 3
Hope Springs Eternal 5
Outpouring of Emotion 6
Two Winding Roads, One Destination 7
Our Best Friend 9
The Visit 11
Checkmate 12
The Great Deception 13
Isn't She Lovely? 14
The Missing Link 15
The New Guy 16
The Birth of a Dream 17
Bless the Child 18
This Is Just the Beginning 19
Twenty-four Hours 20
You Are My New Day 21
Father Figure 22
"Biological" Father 24

SEASON II: SUMMER
Summer Defined 29
The Season 31
I Will Comfort You 32
Happy Birthday 33

A Quiet Example of Leadership 34
What Is Success?. 36
Die for Love. 37
Just Be Ready. 38
A Perfect Recipe. 39
A Real Man 40
Wisdom Is the Key. 41
Who Needs Football?. 42
Sister, Sister 44
In the Clutch 45
My Vision of You. 46
One 47
Fun Love 48
Isn't Love Crazy?. 49
You Can Make It 50

SEASON III: AUTUMN
Autumn Defined 53
They Have Finished Their Course. 55
Death Is Not the End. 57
Should I Give Up? 58
Man of Many Skills 59
The Saltine Tin. 60
Time to Get on the Bus 61
Thank You for the Love 63
I Understand 64
Lean on Me 65
Thank You to My Enemies. 66
Need Him to Survive. 67
Reality 68
Why?. 69
The Eye of the Storm 70
The Big Question. 71

Sailing Through the Storm 72
It Is Our Call 73
The "N" Word 74
Get Back Up When You Fall 76
Three Plus One 77
Smile Again 78
Take America Back. 79
This Is a Special Day. 80

SEASON IV: WINTER
Winter Defined 83
The Color of Anger, the Color of Pain 85
Sniper. 87
Winter's Beauty?. 88
Nobody's Perfect. 89
Can I Just Be Me? 90
Without You 91
Dealing with the Hate 92
At Death's Door 93
My Prayer. 94
The Forgotten One. 95
I Wish I Knew 96
My New Prayer 97
Three Hours Later 98
In Him I Have Enough 99
In Him I Trust 100
The Two Flames 101
How Do You Spell Stress?. 103
Some Things Never Change. 104
My Life, My Death 105
An Endless Journey 106
Is This the End?. 107
Which Way is the Truth? 108

The Closet 109
Death of Desire 110
Hank Gathers. 111
Absentee Fathers. 112
Please Forgive Me. 113
Love Hurts 114
Tomorrow Is Not Promised 115
Where Is My Help? 116
Help Me, Please 117
Life's Lessons 118

Epilogue. 121

Prologue

S - Sessions in
E - Eternity
A - Assigned to
S - Separate and
O - Objectify God's
N - Necessary and
S - Sovereign events

Every point in our lives is governed by the seasons. There is a time and purpose for every event we encounter as we run along our respective courses.

> To every thing there is a **season**, and a time to every purpose under the heaven: A time to be born, and a time to die; a time to plant, and a time to pluck up that which is planted; A time to kill, and a time to heal; a time to break down, and a time to build up; A time to weep, and a time to laugh; a time to mourn, and a time to dance; A time to cast away stones, and a time to gather stones together; a time to embrace, and a time to refrain from embracing; A time to get, and a time to lose; a time to keep, and a time to cast away; A time to rend, and a time to sew; a time to keep silence, and a time to speak; A time to love, and a time to hate; a time of war, and a time of peace.
> —Eccl. 3:1-8 KJV, emphasis added

This book is designed to be the words you may need in whatever season you are in at any time and place. Please take heart, knowing that the situations you may be facing will only last for a short while and help may be just on the next page you turn. Take your time, sit back, and enjoy words that are written just for you in whatever you may be going through; the right words at the right times. "A word fitly spoken and in due **season** is like apples of gold in settings of silver" (Prov. 25:11 AB, emphasis added).

Season I
SPRING

Spring Defined

S - So much
P - Promise one hopes to
R - Realize
I - In a time of
N - Newness and
G - Growth

During this time of year, hope buds everywhere, signaling new life and the birth of dreams. Every single idea seems to be overflowing with good vibes and feelings. Spring is a time for taking new chances to get new opportunities—the anticipation of doing just that, mixed with a little fear of taking such risks. It is a time to chase your dreams and not put them to the side. "Hope deferred maketh the heart sick, but when the desire cometh, it is a tree of life" (Prov. 13:12).

Spring is a time for planting new seeds with the expectation of astronomical growth and prosperity. While you do not see the results of your planting immediately, with faith you will see the hope for the future. "For we are saved by hope: but hope that is seen is not hope: for what a man seeth, why doth he yet hope for? But if we hope for that we see not, then do we with patience wait for it" (Rom. 8:24-25).

Spring is a transitional time that allows us to see what we thought of as negative moments in our lives as opportunities for improvement and restoration. "And the floors shall be full of wheat, and the vats shall overflow with wine and oil. And I will restore to you the years that the locust hath eaten, the cankerworm, and the caterpillar, and the palmerworm, my great army which I sent among you" (Joel 2:24-25).

Just like the lead leg in a relay race, how you handle this season can have dramatic effects on the rest of the year. Start out fast and build momentum heading into the passing of the baton to the next portion of the season's race.

Ghetto Child

In a neighborhood full of chaos, violence and drugs are what you see,
There is a child who lives with this, as their very reality.
A small flower, a girl, maybe even a little boy,
Given guns, knives, and stress as their only ghetto toys.
You see, Daddy left when the little one came
Now he is the blame for Mom working three jobs
Because his game was really lame, and he will just
Move on to another, if with you it is all the same.

A mother is forced to assume both roles,
Required to mold a child with time full of gaping holes
Where she should have been there, but could not,
She was at three jobs, sweat pouring from her brow,
To give that child all that she's got.

The government acts as if it wants to assist,
But as soon as she got a job, they took her name off the list.
What could she do except get another J-O-B,
"Just Over Broke" is all that really means to me.
Bills were coming due, she saw her child only as they slept at night,
She wasn't sure, but she prayed that everything would be all right.

What does the child learn from all of this?
Well, they'll never know the feeling of their father's kiss;
A father-son game, a father-daughter dance will be missed,
And while there is no real man in the midst
Will they take out their frustrations with their fists?

Four Seasons of Verse

The church has to be a place for the mom and child to turn,
Learn and discern the necessary lessons to escape this awful trend.
They need a spiritual father and a very best friend.
Will the doors of the church be open to embrace this precious rose?
Or will the sins of their parents' past keep them from getting in?
Can we stop judging people and just give the love
That God has shown us from above, and hold them tight like a glove?

The church must show the world that it has the key
To take on the hard case so people will know and see
There is a way out of this mess, when God will bless
The child to progress and be able to address
The situation at hand with a plan to move from this land.
Give mom what she never had; repay her for getting through the bad
Times together as one; although all things weren't games and fun.

You're getting out of the ghetto—spirit, body, and soul,
Your eyes are open to the truth; higher education is now your goal.
Physically and mentally—mind, will, and emotions too,
A ghetto child emerged from their cocoon,
And away from the ghetto they flew.

Hope Springs Eternal

A smile so sweet, I swiftly melt when I see it,
Eyes that say so much, they're seemingly a perfect fit.
The first moment she smiled, and looked my way,
I knew at that point, there was something I had to say.

I had to let her know, exactly how beautiful she was,
I just had to tell her too, what her just looking at me does.
And when we talk, her majestic beauty only improves,
It's funny how I am impressed, just by the way she moves.

Her presence brightens my day, whenever she walks in the room,
I think about the very first time, that these emotions began to bloom.
A smile spreads across my face, remembering the feelings then,
For her to look this good, it probably should have been a sin.

I had no idea when, and not a single clue how
I could convey my point, the sweat poured from my brow.
Nervousness set in, I began to have doubts in my mind,
Maybe I shouldn't say anything, and just push the feelings behind.

Then again if I didn't, I guessed I would never know,
Just what might have happened, if I gave it a chance to grow.
What would be the best way, to effectively say what I feel?
How do I word it right, so that she takes me for real?

I might as well just be direct, and see what comes later on,
After she hears what is said, and I am physically long gone.
I hope she understands, that I want to put no pressure in her day,
I just want to be honest; but if she desires, I will get out of the way.

Outpouring of Emotion

Valentine's Day is just one more time to show,
The thing that every day I hope that you know.
One holiday to me cannot begin to compare,
To the daily feelings that with you I attempt to share.

If I buy you a gift on that day you can be sure,
That the emotion behind it is definitely all pure.
It does not have to be a holiday for me to let you see,
That the feelings I have are not accompanied by a fee.

I cannot tell right now just what you really feel,
All I know is to my own feelings that I must kneel.
Every time you look at this fountain as it pours,
Know that inside my heart there is plenty more.

Two Winding Roads, One Destination

Written in honor of the founders of the Christian Fellowshippers bowling league of Flint, MI who dedicated their lives to it and all of us involved.

As the season comes to an end, we can sit back and review,
All the good things we have done, and the things that we didn't do.
We can consider all the strikes, for some few and far between,
The frustrations that sometimes ran deep, if you know what I mean.

We will look at the spares, some splits that made us mad,
Until we reached in our bag of tricks, pulling out shots
    no one knew we had.
When physical ailments tried, to stop some from enjoying the game,
We remember them still going strong, conquering the enemy
    with no shame.

Perhaps most importantly, when we look back on this year,
We will recall the foundation of the league, two people we all hold near.
Mrs. Moore is a true fan; she will make you believe you can fly,
Mr. Moore is a comedian, ready to get you when your ball misses
    the pins and goes by.

Every week without fail, they come with smiles on their faces,
Even when it hurts to walk, they made it there with God's grace.
No matter what, you knew you would have someone cheering
    against your defeat,
And by the time you sat down, that pay envelope would be at your seat.

Everyone on the league was treated, with the same love and care,
Although a few got mocked a little more, when they missed that easy spare.
But it was all done with love, so undeniable to all who could see,
Just like parents to most of us; well, I guess like grandparents to me.

The road that each took, was very different to say the least.
And we can appreciate them both, as we partake of this feast.
One road smooth and straight, the other as jagged as it can get,
From Mrs. Moore's "Good job," to Mr. Moore's "Nothing to it."

These words help express our love, but not just for this year,
For all of the time past, that you've stood behind us to cheer,
Whatever the future holds, as the winds of time go by,
We hope you keep that same sense of humor, when we all
    meet one day in the sky.

Our Best Friend

In our lives you brought out the sunshine,
Even in the midst of a storm,
You made this world feel like it could be ours with time,
With you what was extraordinary became the norm.

Only in our dreams did we think someone like you could exist,
And in reality we found that to be true,
The good you've done for us no one could list,
It was like paradise being with you.

How do we begin to say good-bye?
Sometimes it can be short and sweet,
While other times might be done with tears in our eyes,
But looking forward to the next time we would meet.

What is hard is knowing when that time will be,
And having to live without you now,
Your care for us was as vast as the sea,
We will see you again, we solemnly vow.

There were times when we did some things wrong,
But through it all we knew it was true,
Your love and forgiveness stuck with us all along,
We were blessed that God gave us someone like you.

Four Seasons of Verse

Words cannot even begin to detail,
Exactly what a father means to his sons,
It did not matter how many times we fell,
You were always there to tell us we won.

As we look back on the things of the past,
Our spirits and hearts will begin to mend,
In the meantime we will just have to hold fast,
And remember that you will always be our best friend.

The Visit

I enter into a strange building in a new place,
With anxiety and fear running through my mind,
A masked man begins to reach for my face,
And another one sneaks upon me from behind.

My heart starts to pound and even skips a beat,
My mind whispers to me to get up and run,
For some reason, though, I am paralyzed in the seat,
My legs seem as if they weigh a ton.

Wait a minute; he grabs something off of a tray,
Oh my God, what in the world could it be?
Whatever it is, he brings it my way,
Then I feel numbness come to overtake me.
I realize what's happening when to my other side he flips,
These men are here today, to extract wisdom from my lips.

Going to the dentist can be quite the experience . . .

Checkmate

This life we live is a game of chess,
If you don't know how to play, you'll be in a mess.
The pawns are the little, everyday things,
The joys, the pains, the temptations life brings.

The bishop is your mother, who protects your dome,
Your father is the rook, providing a castle for your home.
The knights are your siblings, who always have your back,
The queen is your significant one who embodies what you lack.

You're the king my friend, so proceed to the front,
Kick away the bad things just like an NFL punt.
Guard your heart and mind against the evil of today,
Get down on your knees every day and pray.

So with sword in hand, take control of your life,
Don't let this world slice you up like a knife.
Pick up your bat and step up to the plate,
Protect yourself and don't end up in checkmate.

The Great Deception

In this time we use to celebrate,
Someone in our lives whom we appreciate,
We have to understand the truth of it all,
We must examine all things whether big or small.

You see, cupid is supposed to fill our hearts,
With all of this love using piercing darts,
And while all this may seem to be great fun and jest,
In reality, cupid is a son born of incest.

What are we celebrating, do we really know?
This illegitimate child shooting arrows with a bow.
To most, getting flowers or candy just has to be,
But the thing that's most important is absolutely free.

If we shared our love during the other 364 days,
Then it wouldn't matter how much our loved one pays.
We would realize that Valentine's Day is just a joke,
Floral shops suck us in and we leave there broke.

Don't let cupid's arrows deceive your mind,
And let this supposed holiday put you in a bind.
If you are stalled just kick yourself in gear,
And make the person you love number one every day of the year.

Isn't She Lovely?

How immaculate her beauty is,
Every man wishes she were his,
From top to bottom, front to back,
There is nothing that she has come to lack.

Her exterior glows and is like silk,
She quenches your thirst like a cup of milk,
She is as beautiful inside as she is out,
Her warmth and comfort leaves no doubt.

She is your queen and you beam with pride,
Every single time you climb in for a ride,
And when people see you, both near and far,
They say, "Man, you sure do have a nice car!"

What did you expect?

The Missing Link

Love is such a hard game to play,
It demands attention every single day.
Some days are harder and may bring pain,
Some shower compassion like a fresh, spring rain.

What's hard is knowing which day will come,
And how to deal with it until the day is done.
What can I do to make that time pass?
When love cuts your heart like shards of glass.

What makes it worth it are those very good days,
When love shines on you with its transparent rays.
All of the heartache is released from your mind,
Knots of pain in your soul begin to unwind.

So, be mindful of love and how to cope,
And don't let it strangle you like a noose of rope.
When love hurts your heart, be sure to think,
The void in your heart will be filled by that same missing link.

The New Guy

Starting a new job is very hard at first,
Nervousness swells up until you are about to burst.
You try to do everything right to impress your boss,
You smile on the outside, but on the inside you're lost.

You try to watch and learn all that you can,
Everyone seems quick to give you a helping hand.
You don't want to ask questions and seem unsure,
But you have problems and need the cure.

You're feeling confused and don't know what to do,
You feel out of place and you don't have a clue.
Just then, someone comes to help you out,
And you see what your coworkers are all about.

As time passes, things will certainly change,
They won't seem nearly so new or so strange.
You'll become comfortable and realize out of the blue,
That this job really needs somebody just like you.

The Birth of a Dream

**Written through the eyes of an expectant
woman awaiting her child's arrival**

A vision begins to run through my mind,
The picture grows clearer as I start to unwind.
I see a day coming that is like no other,
Another step in my life when I become a mother.

I see the long days and pain that I must face,
I see the tired legs from the very strenuous pace.
I see the hard looks from people, who just don't understand,
I see the tears in my eyes; it seems no one will hold my hand.

But then I see the joy of anticipating the day,
The preparations are being made; I am on my way.
I see myself smiling, as I visualize what's to come,
The excitement is so strong, that I almost feel numb.

Then I awake from my daze, and look all around,
All of my earlier agony, is nowhere to be found.
My life will be blessed, no matter how it may seem,
When my baby boy is born, the birth of my dream.

Bless the Child

Don't rock the boat, is what we are told,
Be reserved and quiet, don't be so bold.
Wait your turn, and sit back and learn,
Follow behind us, around every turn.

You're just a child; you have nothing to say,
We had to bite our tongues, keep our feelings at bay.
Clamp down on our thoughts, push back our dreams,
Stop dead in our tracks, and stay off of the team.

But I beg to differ from that, because my mind is vast,
Trying to hold me down, is certainly a thing of the past.
So what I am a child, my wisdom is still great,
You might just find out, if you didn't make me wait.

All that I am saying, is to open up your minds,
I am tired of being in the back, or even left behind.
Listen to the child, and let him out of the cage,
Because children are the only ones, not contaminated by age.

This Is Just the Beginning

In a time when sorrow can mire a soul, and make us not believe,
We need to remember the truth, and the reason why we grieve.
We will miss our loved ones, as they have been laid to rest,
We cherish their memory, as they leave this earthly nest.

This is the most difficult part, trying to find a way to say goodbye,
Asking God for answers, as we turn our gaze up to the sky.
"Why Lord?" we may ask in our search to find the way,
"Why was this precious one taken from us?" is all we can say.

"Their work on earth is done," is what the Lord said one day,
"They have done all that they could, and have outlasted their stay."
Because they left us, before we were ready to let them go,
It left us with a void, filled only with heavy emotions to tow.

All the wisdom they bestowed on us, while God had them here,
Will live forever in our hearts, as we keep their memories near.
It seems every little thing, will remind us of them more and more,
A bittersweet reflection for us, which touches our very core.

The witty humor that defined them, they have passed on to us,
They were as young as they felt, their age they never even wanted to discuss.
All of the many friends, who are supporting the family this day,
Show the impact that they had, as they did things their way.

Their date with eternity and destiny, has arrived on its own cue,
They left the pain and evil of this world, not leaving any one of you.
Don't look at death as the end, just as a means to eliminate their strife,
In fact it is much more than that, it is in essence the true very beginning of life.

Twenty-four Hours

Time . . .

People say that there is not enough of it,
But they seem to "make" time for the things they
Really care about . . .
That makes me wonder, "What is important?"
Will they find a few minutes to tell
Their soul mates that they care?
Or will they decide that the television shows
They are watching demands that attention?

Is seeing that special someone
Worth braving the cold weather to do?
Is going to the mall better than stealing away
For a private phone conversation?
Is spending time with the couch and remote more
Important than quality time with the one you love?

I think not, but I digress . . .

These seem to be all of the questions
That cause couples to have problems every day.
The issues that require more time for an argument
Than it would have taken to avoid them at all cost.
People have to be honest with themselves,
And realize their priorities . . .
Begin to understand that the days with loved ones
Will not last forever as they may feel.
So the only thing to consider as your heart is scoured,
What will you do with your next twenty-four hours?

You Are My New Day

In the opening of a brand new day,
And in the close of a fleeting night,
A slight, crisp breeze flows by my way,
An image of pure beauty enters my sight.

No matter the course from sunrise to sunset,
No matter the trials that I go through,
That breeze reminds me it's not over yet,
And dealing with the valleys is what I have to do.

But trouble certainly won't continue to last,
And a new day will come with the dawn,
I know that soon my turmoil will pass,
And life will no longer use me as a pawn.

That oncoming day brings hope and promise to me,
Even when it seems that I may not have a clue,
Although that wonderful wind is impossible to see,
I am positive that my gentle breeze is you.

Father Figure

A father sitting and imagining the future regarding his sons

Here I sit in the depths of confusion, trying to decipher the pull on my soul
As I look at an image of my oldest son, given my name, my countenance, my heart, and my goals.

My youngest is here, another mini me, what a joy it can be when he is sitting on my knee
And in my eyes he can see, a real man free to be what he is supposed to be.

I have to continue to show them the way, no matter what temptation comes to lead me
Astray or what negative things people may say.

It's hard to not be able to give them everything they want, provide them the things I never had; take away their sad, bad, and mad, leaving glad in its place.

I must stay on the path that's straight so they can see the way to lead their own futures to
The light; keep myself out of trouble and stay in the fight.

Father Figure

I can't be a father from an iron-clad cell, trying to keep another man from posting his bail
With me because he will never again see a female on the outside of the barbed-wire fences from which he cannot flee if you know what I mean.

I have made a decision not to be that way, but rather to be the light that illuminates the road so on the right path they can stay; keeping the urge to stray at bay.

All the fathers out there, I hope your choice is made. Be the true examples you should; keep your bills paid. Encourage your kids to make the grade and not settle for just getting by and lying in the shade.

The next time those children looks up into your eyes, ask yourself, "Do I want to be responsible for their demise?" The time is now to get it right, hold them tight and make sure you never let go. Never make them guess that you love them, but rather make sure they know.

Be a true father figure . . .

"Biological" Father

I know a man, who thus far has yielded no seed of his own,
But yet many look to him when they feel alone
Because their father is gone; he may have
Finished his course on earth or decided the time
Was not worth it at some moment after birth.
Either way it is the adolescent that pays
For so many days and I continue to be amazed
At how resilient the children remain.

They still need a strong male force
In their lives to help steer their course
Helping provide what they're missing from the original source.
That's where this man I know comes into play,
He can and does demand a ban on excuses with what
They say and the misuse of the emotions that
They've kept at bay…

I also know that this man needs more help to reach
All the kids' lives his impact is supposed to breach.
Especially with so many males in jail or in a world that
Feels like a living hell while they fail to bail
Themselves out of the sinking ship of their past;
No hope for the future because everyday they wonder
If their life is going to last or end fast at the sound
Of a gun blast.

"Biological" Father

So men, real men, please step up to the plate and help
These kids escape the fate that many will say has an
Inevitable date; spread the love and wisdom you have gained
From God to retain the youth and help allow them to attain
The goals that they set before, but began to wane due to the stains
Left in their hearts and souls from the void that remains.
Perfection is not needed for it is the pursuit of such that
Means you have so much to give; a calming word and
A delicate touch, but sharp as a knife when you know
Their life is on the line and the small strife will be worth
It in time. I know a man who will appreciate that assist
And kids that push during their uphill climb.

I thank you real, true men.

Season II

SUMMER

Summer Defined

S - Sensational and
U - Unique peak;
M - Making
M - Maximum potential
E - Equivalent to
R - Realized results

This season brings with it a sense of fullness and effervescence. Dreams that were birthed in spring blossom into completeness. Summer is the time for basking in the glow of the longest days of the year and the fairest weather. The fruits of the trees are at their ripest point and it is time to gather food as preparation for the future. "The ants are a people not strong, yet they prepare their meat in the **summer**." (Prov. 30:25, emphasis added).

Wisdom is shown in the way the summer months are handled. It is not a time to allow laziness to creep in. The wise know that colder times are coming and they make accommodations for it. "He that gathereth in **summer** is a wise son: but he that sleepeth in harvest is a son that causeth shame" (Prov. 10:5, emphasis added).

The summer is also a time of success and prosperity realized. It is generally the peak of our existence and we are motivated to keep it with us as long as we can. Love that was birthed in the spring grows into full bloom. "Let thy fountain be blessed: and rejoice with the wife of thy youth. Let her be as the loving hind and pleasant roe; let her breasts satisfy thee at all times; and be thou ravished always with her love" (Prov. 5:18-20).

In this second part of the relay, you are looking to hold on to the lead in life you have established by now. It is often the fastest leg and a mad sprint to reach the halfway point of the year. There is no time for laziness here, but rather a drive that is second to none.

The Season

Christmas in July

It's the time of the year again for us to stand, give thanks to God for the Man
That He sent down to us through His plan.
There is no way we can repay our God for this day, no words that we can say
To make up for Him rescuing us from the fray.

This is also a time to spend with whom you love, also sent from above,
In the form of family and friends who will be there until the end.
It is also a time to reflect on the time past, loved ones lost seemingly too fast,
But their memories will forever last. God help us deal with the pain that remains,
And the utter disdain, let it continue to wane until peace permeates through our veins.

We thank You for that perfect joy, manifested through all of us;
Man, woman, girl, and boy.
Heal our hearts with what we hear, so that we can appreciate the family that
We still have here.

This family has always been and will continue to be for You, in all that we do,
And all that we say in times of serenity and of play.
We thank You for this time and for the years to come, and we will continue to stay
Faithful until our time is done.

I Will Comfort You

I have been sent by the Most High,
To meet and supply all of your needs,
I am here every time you should cry,
Each time that your troubled heart bleeds.

Although you cannot see Me or touch,
Allow your soul and spirit to reach out,
Realize that God loves you so very much,
And sent Me to you so there is no doubt.

No matter what foe or where you must go
I will be there to show you so that you know
I am with you when you are high, or low even more,
So much so that all your burdens I will tow.

Who am I? I am the Comforter sent from above
With love so unimaginable that to try to explain
Would be in vain; I am the One Who will not leave
When you grieve, but rather provide hope and scope
That allows you to cope.
I am here for you no matter how hard things get;
I am the *one and only* fit, for your soul, that is,
The Holy Spirit.

Happy Birthday

As I sit and reflect about the day of your birth,
And all that this day you now mean to me,
I just thank God for putting you on this earth,
And bringing your bright smile for me to see.

There was a time when I didn't fully understand,
I didn't know what being around you could mean,
Then it all seemed to fall out of my hand,
When you were no longer there for me to lean.

They say that you don't know what you had,
Until after it is already gone and past,
Talking to you certainly does my heart glad,
But seeing you would allow that feeling to last.

What I am trying to say is that I wish I were there,
To really enjoy the person you've grown to be,
But maybe one day our company we will again share,
And I'll take advantage of that time, you will most definitely see.

A Quiet Example of Leadership

The word *respect* is tossed around, frivolously from day to day,
But the real definition is personified here, today in this display.
For all who knew him, esteem was automatically the way,
And the smart ones listened and learned, from all he had to say.

Words mean so very little, when the actions really don't coincide,
But when the language and works collide, reverence must then abide.
Quiet leadership defined your plight, even just sitting in your chair,
Reading the Word of God, despite worldly cares that were there.

I can hear so many call you "Daddy," from young all the way to old,
You earned it by providing for so many, rescuing them from the cold.
Children and grandchildren alike, saw you in this reverent light,
A title wrongly placed on so many, but every night you made it right.

This is the real price of respect, putting your own needs in the rear,
Looking out for the protection of many, those both far and near.
But you didn't count up the cost, to account for good will,
You only hoped to instill, to address the voids that we could fill.

As the young sat on your lap, seeking their wants through your good deeds,
You met so many of the cravings, making sure to fulfill their needs.
Yet you lectured as you gave, teaching lessons along the way,
That the path to success is not easy, and one must fight each day to stay.

A Quiet Example of Leadership

A model of consistency at home, married to one for many years,
Bucking against the status quo, persevering through the fears and tears.
Showing the statistics don't have to apply; our unions can indeed survive,
The fifty percent failure rate they claim, can take a serious dive.

Through it all you held firm, as a patriarch illuminating the way,
From your service to God and this country, to keeping the family
    above the fray.
These words of sheer admiration, are to say thanks to God and you,
For Him giving you a plan to lead, and for you to the end seeing it through.

What Is Success?

Another milestone met, another mountain climbed,
The light at the end of the tunnel, the past left behind.
Very few know the true struggles I came through; along the way
To this day, many clouds saturated with rain and so much pain.

Racism overcome so that God's will could be done
Not just on earth, but in Flint you see, despite the economy
He has set me free; and clear from the bondage of disappointment
 and fear.
He let me know that whatever happened, He was still here.

This is not the end; for I have only just begun
My journey under the Son, the race is still not done.
The next step will be God's, ordered by Him alone,
His will for my life can be my one and only goal.

I know this one thing, that without Him nothing is truly real;
The feeling you have when you are truly in His will,
Sacrificing so much for the sake of what's best while not knowing at
 the time;
That is the real price of success.

Die for Love

For love, yes, I am willing to die,
There will be those who question and ask why
Lose your life and go into the sky
Just to get a small piece of love's pie?

To me, love is an unmatched high
And makes me feel as if I could fly.
To the one that I love, I would never lie,
Hopefully she returns the feeling and I would be her guy.
I'd do my best not to make her cry
And a strong bond together we would definitely tie.

We would love one another, while our lives go by,
Fitting perfectly together, as our hearts draw nigh,
She would be the single apple of my eye,
For her I would give up everything, even my life if I had to die.

Just Be Ready

A new year is upon us, much better than the last,
The arrival of a new day, is approaching very fast.
A new millennium, a new decade, and new century will be here,
The Y2K bug after this, no one will ever again fear.

Now the anticipation begins, the hour is getting late,
We know the time is coming, but for now we must wait.
The horns will sound; people's voices will be raised,
In many houses of worship, Jesus Christ will be praised.

Let the festivities start, let all the music play,
All of the bad in the current year, will end on today.
Only one resolution is needed, so let it be known,
You just want to be ready, when the final trumpet is blown.

A Perfect Recipe

I can't seem to put my finger on it,
Truth is, I really don't understand,
There's just something about you,
That helps keep you in demand.

Is it in the way you look,
Or the way you do your hair?
Maybe it's the things you say to me,
Or perhaps the stylish clothes you wear.

I doubt if it is any of those,
They are too superficial to be true,
It has to be something deep on the inside,
The things that show the real essence of you.

The way you smile when I see you,
As well as the little attitude you bring,
Those little things that make you unique,
Like the times when I hear you sing.

It must be a mix of all those things,
Each one of them doing its own part,
That has just got to be the reason,
You have stolen a piece of my heart.

A Real Man

I long for the day when men of all races can be perceived in the same way,
Earn the same pay, but that's definitely not today.
No longer viewed as a thug because my hat is not straight,
My clothes are not tight, and my braids are out-of-sight.

Some people can't seem to see, the 3.89 on my bachelor's degree,
All of things done for humanity, and of course the great poetry.
Why is it no one assumes that I play chess for fun, or when people are in need
I am the one who is called upon until all the bad times are done?

It is those like me who are quick to receive blame, some folks think it's a game,
No matter how much we think things have changed, they still remain the same.
It's been this way since before I was born, but maybe before too long,
The hearts of the world will change and this strife will be gone.

But I doubt if that will be, because hate is encased in the fabric of society,
Will it take until eternity for them to come from behind the façade of supremacy?
Only God knows the true fate of this land, so until my end I must do all I can,
Paying respect to those who do not follow the plan, fighting for that which I believe,
The essence of being a real man.

Wisdom Is the Key

In this life we live, wisdom is the key,
Instead of buying bread, you'll own the bakery.
Not only will you have, a meal for you to eat,
You'll never be hungry, because you will catch your own meat.

You will not only have, a song in your heart to sing,
But you'll have the composer, and happiness new melodies bring.
You will have a gift, maybe in the form of a toy,
But you'll also have the giver, which will bring great joy.

Having the preacher is good, but I will tell you what's best:
Having the Word in your heart, becoming more than just a guest.
You can have new shoes, that you think are gold,
But if you have the maker, your feet will never be cold.

A brand new automobile, will only last for a while,
But a new one every month from the builder, will bring endless smiles.
To have somebody truly love you, will make your heart glad,
But if you have love in your own heart, my friends, you will never stay sad.

Who Needs Football?

It has been said that men can't come together
Without there being discourse or a fight,
At a football stadium, basketball arena,
Or even a dance club at night.
People, I'm here to tell you another tale,
Of thousands of men brought together as one,
Under a single common veil.
That is the covering of God that cannot fail and shall
Keep these men from going to hell,
The eternal jail.
There are football players on stage, but no game being played,
Left fielders in the crowd, but not a swing being made.
Grown men crying their eyes out
Not because the bills are due, or the wife's upset;
The kids are out of control, and their needs aren't met.
But because they're still here and able to actually
Walk free, or maybe just because they have
Come so far from where they used to be.
They laugh with joy like they've never before seen,
They didn't win the lottery, seal a bet, or feel
That their lives were just that pristine.
No, it's because they were able to make it here
Through 500 miles of traffic, or planes being delayed,
Even if they are sitting all the way in the rear;
They are able to stand with the rest
And do their best to stick out their chests,
Pass all of the tests; get rid of life's pests
No matter how far they've come from the east and west.

Who Needs Football?

Oh yeah, men CAN come together as one,
Although getting to the destination may not be all fun.
It is worth it in the end, the power of many men
Will help release those problems that weigh a ton.
In God's stadium is where this all exists,
Such a truly awesome presence in the midst,
Knocking Satan out with power much greater
Than the force of a man's fists.
So don't you be the one to miss this place of spiritual bliss
Where real men join hands on the same page
With no more rage and engage in conversation
About the Lord Whom they heed.
Who needs football?
These men know God is all the entertainment they really need.

Sister, Sister

Sharing the years of our youth, and also years to come,
Seeing the tears that we would cry, knowing where they came from.
Sitting in a small living room, one unit watching TV as a whole,
Slow to anger with each other, biggest argument over the remote control.

Imagining one day as we sat, what life would be like ahead,
Inquiring as to the reasons why, at 10:00 p.m. you always went to bed.
I can't begin to explain, the relationship that has grown,
I know a "half" is what they said, but whole is what we've always known.

Several years in the past, you birthed new joys into our lives,
Shaina came first, but soon Lemuel and Joseph would arrive.
Seeing the children grow up, has been a joy that can't be explained,
Starting out from birth, much happiness from them we've gained.

Together we dealt with the bad, and also enjoyed the good,
Time after time we've looked out, for one another as we should.
Too often with siblings in life, this is just simply not the case,
They grow up with resentment; no smiles ever span their face.

Every time I think about that, I thank God for what we've got,
Even during the stressful times, your phone calls to me mean a lot.
Entering into this holiday season, I reflect with great pride,
Envisioning the things of the past, all of the love I feel inside.

Rest assured that this love will last, until eternity takes over time,
Rendering our past and our present, helpless in its wake behind.
Regardless of what challenges we face, whatever problems may blister,
Remember that I love you Sheila, I could not have a better sister.

In the Clutch

It wasn't long ago, perhaps just a couple of weeks,
The big game was approaching, and George had cold feet.
This game would be tough; they were playing the number one team,
But they could certainly win, if they only had enough steam.

He started out in the game, and ran up the floor,
Next thing you knew, he was pushed right out of the door.
He came back in really mad, and ready to fight,
But then calm came over him, and he played well that night.

He found himself open near the end, and they passed him the rock,
He was fouled once again, and his stomach tied in knots.
He went to the free throw line, and he carefully took aim,
He made the first two, and easily won the game.

The fans in the bleachers erupted, and the crowd rushed down,
You couldn't even see him, with all of the people around.
He had an opportunity, and then he took care of the rest,
George was indeed the hero, and on that day he was the best.

My Vision of You

Kind, sweet, and gentle spirit, yet with a burning fire of aspiration inside,
Kept tucked away in secret, but cannot seem to fully hide.
Keen eye for what is present, and what is yet to come to pass,
Killing stereotypes of what she is, held by people in a great mass.

Even though slight in stature, still very strong indeed,
Enemy to the ignorant, friend to those in need.
Everything around her, speaks of elegance and grace,
Erasing the pain of others, with a meek smile on her face.

Simply stated front, yet truly complex underneath,
Sharing her knowledge with a few, wisdom left to bequeath.
Secure in her own skin, but not afraid to grow,
Secrets tucked away within, for only her to know.

Heart made of gold, although it is tender as well,
Holding fast to emotions, even when they hurt like hell.
Hoping for a brighter day, when the morning should arrive,
Hate for injustices in this life, nevertheless thankful to be alive.

A poem has many words, used to paint a vivid scene,
An original piece of work, crafted with feelings so pure and clean.
Art in the form of rhyme, flowing to the beat of my heart,
Amorous depiction of you, what my soul saw from the start.

One

In this life I will win,
I will be second to none,
I will lead from beginning to end,
Dominating until my work is done.

I cannot accept being number two,
Because that is not in my design,
Staying on top is what I have to do,
I was created with being first in mind.

To me, losing is not even a choice,
I have to be victorious in every race,
When I talk all must hear my voice,
Defeat is the ultimate slap in the face.

This life we live is the greatest game,
And when my clock runs out under this sun,
I will look back down from whence I came,
And know that I finished as number one.

Fun Love

Love can really be a lot of fun,
It will brighten your day like the morning sun.
Although it is as innocent as a nun,
Its power can eclipse that of a gun.

The immense presence of love will make some run,
And to others, it may weigh a ton.
The real ones; however, will stay until it's done,
They will run the race until it is won.

To them it is as hot as a toasted bun,
And it brings great joy like a joke or pun.
In its most sacred form it will even produce a son,
Love may be crazy, but it is also a lot of fun.

Isn't Love Crazy?

Love is sometimes a crazy thing,
It may start out as just a fling,
And the next thing you know you're buying a ring.

A beautiful song in your heart you will sing,
Then you'll hear the wedding bells go ding.
A lovely wife into your house you will bring,
And just like a queen she will have her own wing.

Right by your side is where she will cling
And pray every day that nothing breaks that string
That connects your hearts and souls as you swing.

For if it breaks, it will snap with a ping
And if you hit rock bottom, it will certainly sting.

You will drop to your knees to start praying
For God to start the process of your healing.
Then you'll praise Him and start worshipping
And feel brand new just like it was spring.

Isn't love just a crazy thing?

You Can Make It

As I walk down this road of life,
There are roadblocks of hate, envy, and strife.
Sometimes I may struggle, and maybe even fall,
There are times when I turn, and walk right into a wall.

There are potholes and speed bumps there to slow me,
My way down this road is very hard to see.
But wait, could that be a light at the end?
At long last, could I finally find a friend?

I press toward that light at the end of the road,
No matter how many times I fall or how heavy the load.
And along the way, if I happen to run into you,
We can join hands, and you can make it too.

Season III

AUTUMN

Autumn Defined

A - A time of
U - Ubiquitous fulfillment of
T - The seeds planted
U - Underground;
M - Meant to usher in and
N - Nurture a superior harvest

Autumn is a time of year where the hard work of the spring pays off. It is the moment when you get to reap the results of the seeds you have sown. It signifies the payoff of your diligence, but the crisp night air also is a clear and true sign of the impending winter months. Although the leaves are dying, the earth yielding its fruit reminds us that this is a prosperous occasion. "While the earth remaineth, seedtime and harvest, and cold and heat, and summer and winter, and day and night shall not cease" (Gen. 8:22).

The rain will come to help soften the ground that was hardened by the summer sun in order to make the harvest more pleasant and successful. This is a symbol to show that although precipitation is imminent, things are better than they appear. "Then I will send rain on your land in its season, both **autumn** and spring rains, so that you may gather in your grain, new wine and oil" (Deut. 11:14 TNIV, emphasis added).

The realization of things and people dying around you brings with it a certain sorrow; however, the carryover of good feelings from summer is enough to allow you to push forward. "Why art thou cast down, O my soul? And why art thou disquieted in me? Hope thou in God: for I shall yet praise him for the help of his countenance" (Ps. 42:5).

Four Seasons of Verse

The third quarter of the race is one where you have to avoid losing focus and looking too far ahead or at the competition around you heading toward the finish. It is a time for diligent planning and performance to not squander the efforts of the two that led to this point.

They Have Finished Their Course

"Your work on earth is done," is what the Lord said one day
To our fathers and grandfathers, who had outlasted their stay.
All the wisdom they bestowed on us, while God had them here,
Will live forever in our hearts, as we keep their memories near.

Some of them left us here, before we were ready to let them go,
Their departure time came swiftly, leaving us with heavy emotions to tow.
How we cope with the loss, is the most difficult thing to understand,
How can we continue to go on, without the presence of that great man?

It seems like every little thing, reminds you of them more and more,
And then there are the holidays like this, which shake you down to the core.
A bittersweet day of reflection for some, where you recall the good
    times you had,
The fishing trips or just watching the game, all the things that made
    yours a great dad.

I know some of you are like me, and it is your grandfather whom you lost,
No amount of restitution appears to be fair, when you count up the cost.
Regardless of what you try to do, you cannot get him back,
To fill the void that is left in your heart, someone has to pick up the slack.

That is where our Heavenly Father comes in to play His leading role,
He can put back together the pieces; He will heal your aching soul.
Putting your thoughts in His hands, will repair your troubled mind,
He will occupy the space in your life; get your feelings back in line.

You have to focus on the fact that God has planned our lives from the start,
He knows everything that will happen, every single beat of our heart.
Realize that their lives have just begun, and paradise greets them every day,
They no longer have the pain and sorrow, which used to turn their blue skies gray.

They get to be with the Lord, praising Him daily around the throne,
Believe me when I say to you, that they're much happier now that they're gone.
So when you start to ask, "Why me, Lord?" and you are filled with remorse,
Ask instead, "Why not?" your dad and granddad have just finished their course.

Death Is Not the End

Losing a family unit's backbone, uncovers loneliness and concern,
Particularly in a young one's life, with thousands of things yet to learn.
How do you cope with the thoughts haunting your soul?
Undertones of foul notes crawling through your emotions
And in their routes leaving gaping holes.
Who can explain this slew of confusion and sorrow
That allows for no hope in sight for tomorrow?

I think I may have the key to dealing with death today,
And the trick may be to just see it in a different way.
Date with **E**ternity **A**nd destiny **T**hat ends a temporary **H**ibernation
Is why I believe,
It is a means of getting away from all the evil and strife.
Even still I think that death is much more than that,
Death is not the end, but it is the very beginning of life.

Should I Give Up?

I am not a quitter; I know this to be true,
But it is a hard thing not to do when I am trying to see you.
I know that you said "no," to getting to know you in a different way,
But your friendship is what I miss; seeing you maybe five minutes a day.

I have tried everything possible; my bag of tricks is on "E,"
Maybe the goal for which I am reaching, is not meant to be.
I thought it was a fair compromise, but maybe I misunderstood,
The things you laid out to me, what you wouldn't do and what you would.

I figured that if I were still a friend, hanging out sometimes would be okay,
We could go to dinner or a movie, or maybe just relax one day.
I realize now that may be too much to ask, and have come to understand,
No matter what one may want, he can only play the cards in his hand.

Giving up has crossed my mind several times; I even said I would do it twice,
But then I would see you again, and I would be tempted to again roll the dice.
You would think I had learned, after rolling craps so many times,
But my head and my heart still don't agree; feeling like this has to be a crime.

Man of Many Skills

Grandfather, father, brother, and uncle, only to name a few,
You gave of yourself to us all; there was none quite like you.
Provider, protector, and leader, just to name a few more,
Whenever we needed anything, there was always an open door.

How do we begin to say good-bye, to the captain of this team?
There will never be another like you, even in our wildest dream.
A minister to every one of us, you captured our collective heart and soul,
And to see you again someday, has become our common goal.

You brought the sun into our lives, with a smile illuminating the room,
The precious buds of hope that we had, you helped bring into full bloom.
The good you've done for us, no mere words could even say,
And for blessing all of our lives, we say "thank you" on this day.

We know in our hearts that you are smiling down on us from up above,
Now you see all the lives you've touched, all the people you've shown love.
In reverence of your great memory, we will all grow closer as one,
With one heart we will join together, our unity will be second to none.

As we go about our lives, in this world from day to day,
We promise we will do our best, to honor you in all we do and say.
We remember all the times we had, how you helped us climb life's hills,
And we thank God for giving you to us, you were truly a man of
    many skills.

The Saltine Tin

Every time I came to visit, it was there to welcome me in,
In the very same place, and same spot where it had always been.
On the surface rather simple, but when opened you would find
It was filled with substance, a special treasure inside.

It puts me in mind of you, when I think of years past,
All of the memories that cast long shadows that last and
Move so fast through my brain, as I struggle to maintain
And sustain my joy behind my tears of pain.

Since I was born, bacon and rice sandwiches had become the norm
Whenever I would hear the alarm's horn and rise in the morn.
I would wake into your quiet embrace, a show of your grace
That welcomed me into this place with the smile on your face.

Your meek and gentle heart, is no longer with me here,
And although I will miss you dearly, I know there is nothing to fear.
There is no more pain and no more sorrow for you to bear,
You are reunited with your husband, who preceded you there.

This season has taught me to show my family the love, which is truly
    sent from above
To ensure that we fit like a glove as you soar over us like a dove.
I will trust God to lead the way, for assistance in keeping my grief at bay
And to give me the words to say, to help my family know things are okay.

Just like all of the crackers, that were always there to eat for us,
Your spirit remains here; retaining it in our hearts is a must.
While your body was here, rest assured you did all you could do,
I will always remember that saltine tin, and I will always love you.

Time to Get on the Bus

When you think about inhumanity, what really does your mind see?
To most of us I can figure, it's not a full dose of reality.
You say you don't understand, well I will tell you how I feel,
I'll give it to you straight and not pull any punches; always
    keeping it real.

If you believe racism is over, I would advise you to look again,
Many women still clutch their purses at the sight of a black man.
Then there are the police, and while some of them are good,
Others still harass people of color, for being in the "wrong"
    neighborhood.

"Look at Affirmative Action," is what some people may say,
"There are more minorities than ever, getting good jobs today."
I'll say then, "That is true, but also consider this reply,
Just how many of those businesses were they able to buy?"

The sad thing is the fact, that women may even have it worse,
For such a long time, being female was treated as a curse.
And now as they battle, to claw their way ahead,
Some men push them down, viewing them as objects instead.

Take this also into account; I want you to really listen,
Some people are ostracized, just for being Christians.
There are the hate crimes, and churches being burned at night,
May I ask what happened, to our Constitutional rights?

We cannot do anything to change our colors; we were born that way,
The same thing goes for gender, job performance should determine pay.
Can't we worship God, without the worry of coming up lame,
Or watching our sweat and tears, go up in a mountain of flames?

Discrimination is still prevalent in our society today,
And it will go on forever, if we don't change our ways.
Although many may look different, they're in the human race just like us,
Because on this road and walk of life, we all have to ride the same bus.

Thank You for the Love

I thought that losing my grandma, would be the lowest point in my life,
I was only twelve years old then, and the pain cut me like a knife.
No words were able to escape my lips, tears I could not even cry,
I just knew there was nothing worse, than a child forced to say good-bye.

But then some ten years later, death came again to rear its ugly head,
Not to tamper with my grandma this time, but my granddad instead.
He took my grandmother's hand, escorted by her lead,
And at his final celebration, my poetic words I was compelled to read.

Now both the king and queen, of my family were gone home,
From that point free from pain, with brand new mansions to roam.
I knew that although their bodies were gone, their legacy still remained,
But I also understood just knowing that alone, would not stop the pain.

I wondered what I could do, to help fill the existing empty space,
I felt like I had been given great love, only to have it slap me in the face.
My emotions were in shambles; my thoughts had no flow,
The reasons why this happened, I guessed only God would know.

Soon after that I realized, that a plan had been set into place,
The wheels of life were put into motion; I again felt a warm embrace.
Two people who barely knew me, gave my feelings a new start,
They welcomed me into their lives; they opened their collective heart.

I doubt that Mr. and Mrs. Paulk, are fully aware of what they have done,
Inviting me into their home, making me feel again like a grandson.
Thank you for the love and care, and all of the small things you do,
And in this trying time of the year for me, that love will certainly help
   me through.

I Understand

It is said that no one feels the pain that you are going through,
But I want you to know that I do.
No one knows how the sorrow grows and mows through your heart,
But I want you to know that I do.

No one feels the sensation so intense that you don't think you can make it through,
But I want you to know that I do.
Who can comprehend a soul that no seamstress can mend?
I want you to know that only I do.

I have been through the pain of losing a loved one so close,
I have felt the sting of sacrificing the One whom I loved most.
It's a terrible feeling to have someone who had done no wrong taken away,
A feeling so low that even I had nothing left to say.

You can lean on Me because I alone have the key,
To escape all of the hurt, the pain, and the misery.
Who am I? The only One who is in possession of the master plan,
I am the Lord thy God, and it is I Who understand.

Lean on Me

When pressure seems to push you down,
With a force like you've never seen,
All the day long all you can do is frown,
It seems you never have a shoulder on which to lean.

Nothing you do turns out right,
All of your efforts seem to fail,
Everything is a struggle that leads to a fight,
You begin to think you are living in hell.

Take heart and don't give up hope,
You have so much still to live for,
Don't let these things tie you down like rope,
And subsequently contaminate your core.

Keep the faith and continue to pray,
Don't stop smiling no matter what you see,
Tomorrow will bring a brighter day,
And if not, you can still lean on me.

Thank You to My Enemies

To all of those who came up against me,
Always saying that a nobody is what I would be,
Writing me off without a hope or a prayer,
Jealousy causing them to hate me when I'm there.

Wishing me dead or maybe somewhere very close,
Interested in my life probably more than most,
Never acknowledging the fact that is obviously true,
Not wanting to admit that I'm just better than you.

All I have to say is don't pass on by just yet,
Where I am now is not as good as it is going to get,
Just wait and see while I am going through this storm,
When the sky clears I will be way above the norm.

Thanks to you all for keeping my vision clear,
Helping me to stay focused away from drugs and beer,
You'll realize that you didn't have good sense,
And your pride will be subject in the future to this prince.

Need Him to Survive

I saw two new beginnings today; one filled with joy and glee,
The other covered in shock and awe of catastrophe.
One life joined to another in holy matrimony,
One life joined with God forever in eternity.

Understand this fact, departing earth starts us anew,
It is only the beginning of our heaven's view.
Short is the time that we have down here,
Cherish every moment with those you hold dear.

A new couple exchanged vows today as well,
Also in the sight of God, promises made without fail.
The official knot tied, the genesis of a new family,
Two roads converged into one, an expressway of unity.

Amazingly, these opposites are truly parallel lines,
Both new experiences for all, yet with perpendicular signs.
Bittersweet thoughts permeate my mind, both subdued and alive,
Blessings to both families, they'll all need God to survive.

Reality

The time has come for this loved one to leave,
And reach his final resting place.
But the memories remain for us to cleave,
And fill the now empty space.

We must face the truth that he is happier now,
With God; gone from all of the strife.
The reality is he's already shown us how,
To join him later and succeed in this life.

Now it is up to us . . .

Why?

Why don't people really comprehend and understand
The power that God has placed in their hands?
Why is it that people don't really see
That God desires us to walk faithfully?

Why don't people seem to care?
Do they believe that God is unaware?
Why can't people simply just believe
In the power that we have already received?

Why don't people depend on the Word?
Aren't we more important than those little birds?
Why is it that people can't seem to do right?
They put up a façade at service, but party all night.

Why don't people know what they've done?
They have led people astray just for a little fun.
Why can't people see where this will end?
They'll send people to hell who thought they were friends.

Why?

The Eye of the Storm

Having to deal with departure and loss,
Is such a difficult task to do,
When you have to count up the cost,
You realize exactly what you have to go through.

No matter how long they've been with us,
The feelings are still the same,
Your heart feels as if it's been run over by a bus,
And you try to find someone to blame.

Some find a way to blame themselves,
And put their minds through a great deal of stress,
They place their problems up on shelves,
And wonder why they are in this mess.

Others try to put the fault on God,
Inquiring just how He could let this be,
Not understanding that is just a façade,
Hopefully these words will help them see.

As for the burden on them that weighs a ton,
And this struggle that has interrupted their norms,
The Lord is not the One who caused this to be done,
But He will be the One to guide you through the storm.

The Big Question

Love is great when it is not planned,
And you take walks on beaches of jet black sands.
You won't go anywhere without holding that hand,
You announce your feelings all over the land.

But what happens when the newness wears down;
When that smile on your face turns into a frown?
You feel your mate is jerking you around,
And you spread your displeasure all over town?

You hope what you built is worth more than that,
And your now emaciated relationship will soon again become fat.
You pray that what began with the quickness of a cat,
Will not end just as quickly at the drop of a hat.

Now you must overcome this seemingly impossible task,
You wonder if what you want is too much to ask.
In the glorious splendor of the beginning you long to bask,
Now you are left to figure out, "Was it all just a mask?"

Sailing Through the Storm

I wonder if bad things just sit
And lurk underneath the good.
It seems like every time you smile,
There is a scowl waiting to reveal its ugly face.
Does it have to be this way?
Does pain have to fill this empty space?

I do believe that good attains victory
Over evil in the end,
But the blows that evil deals you leave bruises
That may take years to mend.
What can speed up the healing process?
Love, my friend, is the most powerful tool
And the one with the highest success.

You may wonder how love can help you
When you are feeling ignored like
The times you feel as if your emotions
Are in last place on the leader board.
Well, the power of love is as strong as death itself,
And that is enough to make me hold on
Until I make it through the storm.

It Is Our Call

I believe it's true that love never fails, but I also know the human
Flaws in the details that can certainly cause it to derail.
Giving in so that she can win is a thing I have learned to do,
But the reciprocal has yet to ensue and I am stuck in this glue
Because the feelings I have yet reign; however, doubt starts to gain
As I struggle to maintain and wonder can I ever be enough?
Will my pursuit of personal perfection be too slow and her road too rough?

Only time will tell if I will fail to deliver or if I will pale
In comparison to her ideal male. Until then I must continue to hold fast
If I truly want this to last and this relationship not be a thing of the past.

You would think after all this time I would know how to show
Her exactly what is in my head, but instead I seem to be the foe and left to
Tow the dread in my bed, thinking about all she has said.

It is funny how just when I thought I knew and our skies were blue,
A storm in the form of belittlement caused my glee to flee and
Depart from me; is this how it always will be? How can
Two walk together except that they agree?

I realize that what I thought I knew, I don't. What I thought
I would do, now I won't. I give God a call because He is
The Master of all, but He reminds me that He gave us those
Free wills so we could choose not to trip and fall
Over our own issues, both the big and the small.

It is up to us . . .

The "N" Word

Shaking my head from side to side was all I could do…
Stunned, my colleague had the gall to utter a word we all know exactly
What damage it could do; a word that only yields casualties in its wake;
There would be none present rescued from this awful quake.

I know, I know, I'm supposed to be the victim here
Because my skin tone is different from the rest and still invokes fear.
And it's true that in 2009 that there is no way I should have heard
    this line,
But I'm far from the only one who found peace of mind hard to find.

There were two others that heard and though they are lighter than me,
They were also victims because human beings are all I see.
Where are these countries called "White" and "Black" that we refer
    ourselves as,
Or do we just run from the light due to our lack and fear of
    understanding
What is truly right? Why can't we be called Americans, simply
One and the same, instead of calling ourselves invented hate names?

Then there was the source of the utterance, the perpetrator of human
    civil rights,
He is a casualty of his own oversight in dealing with the feelings of his
Past; not ridding his heart of the evil that lasts past the test of time
Even until today; still making excuses so it doesn't have reason to go away.

The "N" Word

I pray for this guy and others like him, that they might flip the switch
Of knowledge from within and cleanse themselves from this terrible sin.
Until that time I will continue to make waves by uncovering the possibilities
That put my forefathers in their graves; crashing right through the glass that
Says that I can only go so far and letting my light shine, but with God as the true star.

Get Back Up When You Fall

Another day comes to a bittersweet end,
One more time for my heart to mend.
A little bit of fear runs through my mind,
Should I just leave this situation behind?

Why do I keep hanging myself on this tree?
Why do I let this same thing continue to bother me?
Don't I know that it just doesn't feel very good?
Things aren't changing; did I think they would?

I guess I go out on a limb to get to the fruit,
But sometimes that tree is cut down to the root.
It hurts when you fall, but I need to get back up,
And be optimistic because half-full is my cup.

I know that one day that limb won't break,
I hope it happens soon for my own heart's sake.
Let this be a lesson to everyone one and all,
To get what is good, sometimes you may first have to fall.

Three Plus One

A man who was much more than just someone I knew,
More than just a handyman, who could fix anything for you.
More than the comedian, who told jokes to get us by,
Far more than the man, who hated to wear a tie.

I cannot help but sit here, and ask the Lord why,
My God, why do good people, seem to be the first to pass us by?
Why is it that when it rains, it always seems to pour,
And the time you've spent with them, leaves you wanting more?

He answers me and says, "My child, his job was done,"
"He has finished his course, and his race has been run."
I understand that I can't be selfish, and that his pain was great,
So his going home, had to be his most desirable fate.

I just would like to take this time, just to let Doug know,
That he means so much more to me, than these words could ever show.
We've shared so many laughs, and watched many basketball games,
We'd cheer for the same teams; we even have the same middle name.

You and your lovely wife, have accepted me for who I am,
And I promise to take care of your girls, the very best that I can.
But I am here to tell you, the number of your kids is really three plus one,
Because after you had your three girls, you found in me an extra son.

Smile Again

The intense pain and agony of knowing
That the one you love you cannot have
Is one that can be felt in the spirit and the soul.
Sometimes you want to just give up and restart
But you can't; the memories are embedded too deep
In your heart.

What can you do?
Can you wait and pray that with time all
Wounds will heal?
Or are you forced to forget the dream of
Finding a mate to meet your ideal?
Furthermore, can your heart and mind recuperate
From this raw deal?

To be honest, I just don't know . . .
Only you can determine the imprint your feelings
Are going to make.
Only you can embrace the path that your destiny
Is obligated to take.
So take heart, smile again; all is definitely not lost,
In the end your patience will grant your innermost
Desires, no matter what the cost.

Take America Back

Our great country was rocked, shaken like a leaf,
People were weeping, and screaming through clenched teeth.
Two of our tallest buildings, were brought to the ground,
Our mouths fell collectively open, left without a voice to sound.

Our government as well, was damaged by these acts,
The Pentagon was targeted, and they're still sorting all the facts.
They used our own machines, planes abused as sticks of dynamite,
Hitting their targets with precision, freezing the nation with fright.

There was one plane, though, that on its way hit a pause,
Thanks to some brave souls, who sacrificed their lives for the cause.
Who would do such a thing, whose heart can be that hard?
Osama Bin Laden, they say, is the one who played that card.

Now there is this disease called Anthrax, putting us on our heels,
A white powdery substance, contaminating our mail when it's sealed.
Is this Bin Laden again, some would argue that it is so,
However, most people are just scared, and don't really know.

Our president has had enough, and sent our troops in to fight,
To locate the culprit, and bring justice to light.
We pray for their lives, while we wait with much care,
Believing that our God, will be with them there.

Tragedy helps us appreciate our families, our husbands, and wives,
But we cannot live in fear, for the duration of our lives.
America has got to move on, and we need to get on track,
We must face our demons, and take our country back.

This Is a Special Day

When this day of the year comes, we remember the past,
The good and the bad, when we saw grandma last.
I guess she would be a mother to some, but you can catch my drift,
This is a day and time for most, only the Lord Himself can uplift.

But how soon we forget, an enormous reason to be glad,
On this day was birthed, the union between Mom and Dad.
A special person was created, brought to us by God,
A person who is true, not showing us a façade.

It is a little more difficult for her, to deal with this day,
Memories resound in her mind; it's hard to keep them at bay.
A bittersweet time of the year, is what she must endure,
When it should be all good, a time when her joy should be pure.

We need to make this day, a joyful experience for her,
To embrace her with warmth, as if she was wrapped in fur.
This poem is a start, of the celebration of Aunt Barbara's life,
To end the period of time, when this day is filled with misery and strife.

We need to show our aunt and sister, the love and honor she deserves,
And do what our example did, not keep our feelings on reserve.
I love you, Aunt Barbara, and appreciate all you've done for me,
And remember through this time, Grandma showed us all the key.

She showed us how to love!

Season IV

WINTER

Winter Defined

W - Waning
I - Images of
N - Nature's beauty;
T - Turning into vague
E - Expressions that threaten to
R - Ruin prosperity

Winter can be a time of desolation and the season in which nature perishes at its greatest rate. Feelings of sadness fight the good thoughts of the year in an effort to come in and reign over this period in our lives. "And pray ye that your flight be not in the **winter**" (Mark 13:18, emphasis added).

However, one should remember that the winter season was set in place as a boundary to mark the end of the year. For there to be an extreme heat of summer, there must also be an extreme cold to bookend each other. "Thou hast set all the borders of the earth: thou hast made summer and **winter**" (Ps. 74:17, emphasis added).

We have to remember that preparations for the spring in our lives begin even in this misery. We must always look to the upcoming, brighter days ahead of us and not get trapped inside the mental anguish of these troubled times. The harvest will come around again; just be patient. "The sluggard does not plow when **winter** sets in; therefore he begs in harvest and has nothing" (Prov. 20:4 AB, emphasis added).

It is imperative that we don't let the desolation of the winters in our lives negatively affect the rest of the time we have. If we accept the fact that the winters are coming, then we can in turn prepare our hearts and minds to face the hurdles head-on and finish the year's race. This is the anchor leg in the relay, which is the one that brings the race back to the starting line. Most would say it is the most difficult leg, but at the end the payoff more than makes up for the hard times.

The Color of Anger, the Color of Pain

Red is all I can see at this moment in time,
A blur runs across my face as memories scramble my mind.
Red is the color of blood that boils over in my veins,
As the intense heat of pain is too real to even feign.

Red is the fire that burns in the cauldron of my soul,
A pit so deep that hell seems to be its only foe.
Red is my heart that has been severed into many pieces,
As reality grinds it up underneath its huge feet.

Red is the passion that once encapsulated your spirit,
Transferring to me as we lived with each other in it.
Red is the sign that I have run into in the road,
"*Stop*, I have nothing to say," is what I'm being told.

What did I do to deserve for it to happen like this?
Were all of the "I'm sorrys" you said meaningless?
How can you fix your tongue to say a certain thing?
In your heart you knew exactly what this weekend would bring.

Can you even tell me how long this has been going on?
Was it that night at the party when I noticed something wrong?
That very night you attacked me for no apparent reason,
Was that the signal to the coming end of my season?

Maybe it's time that I just decide to give up,
Because it seems you've already beaten me to that cup.
That very goblet of defeat is one I thought I'd never see,
Then again I never thought you could do this to me.

If you had been honest from the start at least I could've known,
That my existence in your life you had outgrown.
I'll leave you alone now; my heart can't take anymore,
And to the lock on your heart, I'll leave my key at the door.

Sniper

Crouched above on a darkness-covered roof,
An assassin patiently lies in wait,
Seeking out the next victim of his wrath,
The next one to reach their inevitable fate.

Does he know in advance whom he kills?
Or does he just decide on the fly?
Which man, woman, or child would
Be the next innocent one to reach the sky?

In his heart he begins to laugh,
And in his mind he begins to say,
"Those people will never catch me,
Maybe I will even strike during the day."

More motivated and much bolder he became,
But then suddenly his plans went awry,
The authorities caught this fiend,
Maybe now he will be the next one to die.

Winter's Beauty?

Most people see barren trees, with their branches blanketed beautifully with snow,
Or the ice on a pond, gracefully moved upon by those with skates covering their toes.
They are witnesses to the smiles of the families, who prepare Thanksgiving's meal,
And come together as one, giving thanks for all the love and care they feel.

They see snowmen being constructed, by the tiny fingers of a child,
Or in the now-naked forest, animals running in the wild.
All of the things seem fair, especially with Christmas now on the way,
Presents and songs fill the air, and soon the hope comes on the new year's first day.

But I see a different picture, one with an astonishing opposing view,
One with slippery streets and sorrow, expectations that away the wind blew.
I see my brother lying on a stretcher, the day before our school's Christmas break,
Having a seizure during class, his trembling still to this day makes me quake.

Then I hear my cell phone ring, right in the midst of taking a test,
Telling me to get home soon, my only granddad will soon be laid to rest.
For all of winter's glory and magnificence, and the joy to most it may bring,
All I can do is reflect on the past; I know I cannot wait until it is spring.

Nobody's Perfect

Am I perfect?

Nobody's perfect, this I know,
But it's still a hard fact to live down.
You feel like a huge disappointment
Whenever your mistakes turn others' smiles around.

Will you be looked at any differently?
Can you walk by without being looked at like a bum?
Can you be treated as an equal again?
Or are you doomed to live a life plagued with inferiority?

As you stare down the gun barrel of what you've done,
You begin to realize now that you can't go back.
Was what you did really that bad?
It's pretty sad, everyone around you is mad,
Can this be the worst error you've had?

You feel as if you will choke, it's hard for you to even cope;
Once a brilliant star, you are now a flawed, blurry image
Of what you used to be . . .
Taking responsibility is a must to start rebuilding people's trust,
Is this the end, or just the beginning of redemption from your sin?

Can anyone help me?

Can I Just Be Me?

I'm in the prime of my life, just trying to be my own man,
Many people telling me what to do, while they really don't believe I can.
"Do this with yourself," they say, "and do that with your life,"
Pretty soon I do believe, they'll tell me who should be my wife.

I suppose some of it is my fault, I brought a portion onto myself,
Because I put a pause in my life, and shoved my dreams up on a shelf.
"It is only temporary," I say, but it doesn't seem to get through,
I spend too much time defending myself, when I shouldn't have to.

I thought that I could change, the perception of what people see,
But now I see that I was wrong; what they think will just have to be.
"What about me, Lord?" is the only thing I can cry.
But is that just self-pity? Am I telling myself a bunch of lies?

Even when I am feeling good, someone finds a way to shoot me down,
I'm excited about one thing, then end up feeling like a clown.
My life is killing me on the inside; my heart has no more glee,
Nobody seems to know what I am going through, but can I just be me?

Perhaps not . . .

Without You

A sunny day just isn't the same; all my clouds seem filled with rain,
The wind that's blowing seems too hard, my destination appears too far.
It's a shame how time won't heal these wounds and grooves in the pits of
My heart and soul, so many memories inside this big hole.
My song no longer has a melody, no chords playing in harmony with my
Feelings; an empty note left in its place left to embrace the past,
Full of unfulfilled desires mired in a bog of quicksand sinking so fast.

How did things get this way? What role did I play in the demise of this
Portion of our lives? I wonder if I can escape the pain that remains inside.
Two roads in the woods that may never cross, lost in a forest of space in
My mind; trapped back in time when our paths had rhythm and rhyme.
How do I breach this canyon of grief? My emotion shaking like a leaf in
The winds of change. So strange to have my whole life rearranged like a
Riddle with no clue; doom and gloom reign supreme in my
    nightmarish dream.

I need you to come back to our first love, the one sent from above
    when we fit
As tight as a glove and peace hovered over us; no muss, no fuss, and
    so much trust.
Inseparable is what we used to be, fleeing from the trials of life that
    wore us down
Together pounding our problems into mounds of dust; not just
    empty, listless lust. Everyone says you can't go back and replay the
    past, the things that have happened
Will last and you must start with a new cast. I'm not so sure, but you
    tell me . . . is what was stuck in the past, and what could've been
    never to be?

Dealing with the Hate

I should have known . . .

I used to wonder how it felt to be constantly under attack,
Unfortunately, now I believe I may now know.
When you are on top people try to stab you in the back,
But in your face they put on a fake show.

When there is money involved things only get worse,
And jealousy rears its terribly ugly head.
Making me angry to the point I think I could curse,
All over the lies that some spiteful people said.

You would think if you come to work with a good attitude every day,
Things wouldn't have a chance to get so bad.
But you still get accused by the words people say,
Afraid to admit they can't compete; it's really sad.

I am a grown man and don't have time for work games,
Or having these people around me acting as children do.
I thought everyone in this office felt the same,
But now I realize some get mad when they're not as good as you.

If anyone has an issue with me just let me know,
Be an adult and say it to my face.
I will deal with it then instead of dealing with this all-time low,
I just thought things would be different in this place.

. . . prejudice exists everywhere.

At Death's Door

Once again I weep, with thoughts of what is to come,
Realizing where I am at, tied with memories of where I came from.
Everything at this point, seems so far out of place,
I can no longer painfully force, a smile upon my face.

Seemingly all at once, things continue to pile on,
Every single day, all day, even to the new dawn.
The burden upon my shoulders, feels too great to bear,
I am perishing internally, and no one seems to care.

Perhaps still one day, I will make it out on my own,
And with enough time given to me, my pain will be all gone.
But if it doesn't happen soon, I just may not make it,
Because without actually dying, I'm as close to death as I can get.

My Prayer

What was once a dream, is now a harsh reality,
Darkness looms within my soul, pain arises inside of me.
I once thought I knew what agony was, but it was just a fake,
I know now more than ever, and it may be more than my heart can take.

I cannot even begin to explain, the innermost thoughts of my mind,
Memories are racing through my head, peace I cannot find.
How do I make it stop? How do I control the way that I feel?
Right now I don't know, it seems like I've just had my last meal.

Lord, I am going to really, really need your help this time,
The present situation dictates, that my heart has stopped on a dime.
Please lend me some guidance, and help me through the night,
Because if you don't Lord, I may never be all right.

This is my prayer . . .

The Forgotten One

I am sitting here in this room all alone,
Trying to call you, but no one's at home.
I guess I will just have to sit and wait
To talk to you and touch the hand of fate.

It seems that when I call you're always gone,
Sleeping, busy, or perhaps just avoiding the phone.
When will I get a chance to hear your voice?
When will you allow my heart and mind to rejoice?

I just want to say that I miss you and say that I care,
It's frustrating sometimes to call and only silence is there.
But what is worse is when you are at home,
Yet you are too busy to even talk on the phone.

I don't get to see you, so I try to call,
Without the phone we would have no communication at all.
Sometimes I want to give up and start all over again,
But right now I can't picture you as just my friend.

In my heart there is too much love and care for that,
I cannot just shake these emotions at the drop of a hat,
It is a tough battle, a fight that I fully intend to win,
Therefore, despite the struggle, I must press on until the end.

I Wish I Knew

When it was written that a man wouldn't be accepted in his own home,
Why did I think that it didn't include me?
Truth is, it is far more of a reality than I ever wanted it to be.
So many things going through this dome; memories roam
To just a short time ago; I realized why sorrow has been my hope
For my tomorrow . . .

I am trapped in a box, unable to move freely; no, not a physical one
But rather the voice inside me, the true essence of my being.
Stifled at every turn of the truth by those who refuse to hear,
Yes, by even the one whom I hold most near and dear.

I find myself asking why, even though I really should not,
Someone has to be persecuted by Satan's plot for them to give up
What they've got; submit to the strain of impending pain and
Let all of their efforts wane from the weight of utter disdain.

No matter how big or small the truth is, it still hurts one and all
Down to the bare fiber of their cores, and they seek to settle the score
By launching jabs like daggers even more than before.
Can I withstand the darts that continuously fly my way when I
Have something I feel is important to say? Or will the sores
Bore a hole from my heart through my soul?

I wish I knew . . .

My New Prayer

Immediate future placed in the hands of a man,
A judgment call with no evidence on demand.
Placed in a situation of pause
By a man who decided it was his cause
To step in the path of righteousness for his own sake.

Now having to press on through the tribulations of the time,
Having committed no fault or crime,
But yet paying for merely the claim, much more than a dime.

As a son I must watch my mother grind,
Struggling to find justice and truth with those whose minds
Have been infiltrated and inflicted with lies.

How do I remove the ill feelings from my heart?
Revive the faith that I once had
That a man would do his part,
To help his brothers and sisters succeed from the start?

God, I need some help with all of this
As I can't do it on my own
Cause I may be prone to anger and wrath;
Please help me get on and stay true to the right path,
This now is my prayer . . .

How do I look at the man responsible for the pain
And say that everything is okay?
How can I go on this day to the next
Without my flesh climbing in the way?

Lord, help me . . .

Three Hours Later

Waiting patiently for a familiar face,
Yet none seems to appear,
Nothing around you but empty space,
No familiar voices to hear.

Standing in a room with many but still alone,
No place to sit until the next move comes,
Everyone said by now you would be gone,
Entertaining yourself with a song you hum.

Finally, you are herded like sheep to the next room,
If your name is not on the list embarrassment looms,
You get to the front and tell her your name,
She flips through five pages, but the blank expression remains the same.

"Stand to the side," were the instructions given to you,
"When the coordinator comes, she'll know what to do."
Three hours after you got there you couldn't take anymore,
You would have given your right arm to get out the door.

So here you are outside full of more emptiness and shame,
Writing these words to no particular name,
Wondering how much longer this event will last,
You wouldn't be surprised if another three hours passed.

In Him I Have Enough

It's funny how things go bad when all seems so good,
Funny how an ill-timed word can be so misunderstood.
Despite success all around, problems lurk in the empty space,
Issues of negativity arise, smacking me right in the face.

I've tried to be the best man, that anyone can find
I go to work every day, give back when I have the time.
The moment I think I have finally found the way,
Destructive things come to me, keeping happiness at bay.

I used to think I knew, what joy in life really meant,
Used to tell people I knew, examples from the time I spent.
Now I know the truth, that one can never master this thing,
All your life is just a practice, until the time you can truly sing
About the freedom in the heavens, no more crying there,
No more arguments and fights, peace will rule the air.

Until that time comes, I guess I have to maintain,
Keep doing what I have to do, gaining altitude like a plane
While my enemies wane, and I keep from going insane.
Leaning on God is the master plan, and soaring when I can,
But humbling myself on the other hand, letting Him be the man.
Although the road is rough, situations may seem tough,
I will keep moving forward, for in Him I truly have enough.

In Him I Trust

I experienced something for the first time today,
A wedding anniversary brought rain my way
In the form of droplets from my eyes;
My own personal rainy skies…

It made me ponder on things from the past
That I tried to forget; stuff that happened so fast
That I wondered where it went; Satan surely won that round
But the final bell will not sound until my victory is sent
From above and my opponent lies face up on the ground.

Another thing is true that came from all of this,
I saw living proof of the human nature's resilience
And ability to bounce back in the midst of attack
When hope fades to black; staring in the face of lack.
I was witness to a woman who went through and lost so much
Yet still is able to produce a gentle touch
When there is a need for such a person to clutch.

Today I saw all the things that occurred before,
Still seeing a man with a rotten core
Wishing for God to bore a hole into his soul;
Letting him reap what his sowing put him in store for.
I guess that is up to God, so I must sit back and refrain
From doing it my way, giving him my harvest of pain.
I'm waiting on the scales of justice to re-adjust,
But until then, in Him I will just have to put my trust.

The Two Flames

I thought I knew stress until it showed me its true form,
In the shape of a relationship that is out of the norm.
Blinded by love thought to be sent from above, yet
Caught in a wave that could send even the brave to an early grave.

A candle lit on both ends, but which will burn faster? It depends
On the day and the time with no known reason or rhyme,
Each tomorrow appears to bring a different crime.

On one hand the woman placed on a pedestal up high, no one could deny
The love so strong I thought we could fly. At the opposite end a woman with no time,
To listen to my problems that may arise, or to reach a negotiated compromise.

One flame brings heat when we meet the cold, and brings light when the dark has hindered our sight. The other burns to the third degree, seemingly so difficult for
You to see, but so deep that I continue to lose sleep.

Too tired to hear about my job, a place that threatens to rob me of all the
Energy that I even have left to bob…and weave around the corporate
Anxiety, stress, and strain that constantly troubles my brain.

Which flame will burn the hottest remains to be seen, but in the meantime I have no pillar
On which to lean, can you see what I mean? Right now the bad is taking over by force,
Leaving the good on a collision course with remorse.

No words can tell the swell of tears in my eyes to subside; no audible sound seems
To set loose the bound caverns of my soul, a place with a hole so vast that there is no way I can last and the past catches up to me so fast.

No apology for inflicted sorrow that ruined my hope for tomorrow; no regret for the
Injuries sustained from a disparaging cloud that has rained upon me grief like no other
Before; the thief that has bored a hole and gouged a sore.

One flame so dim it can barely be seen without a keen eye trained to see despite the tears
I cry; can this one be nurtured back into the lead to be the voice that our hearts will heed? Or is the need too great to perform this good deed?

Two flames burning at opposite ends, the one that wins I guess depends on whichever can
Send its energy first; the one that quenches my thirst and quest for that burst of love that I used to feel. Lord, please let that flame be the one that I know is real and close this deal.

Please?

How Do You Spell Stress?

What is stress?

Set up for failure at every turn, not knowing who will be next to try to burn
You; trying to use it to gain themselves some points they have not earned.

Trapped like a rat in a world that is fat, stuffed with pride and gall all used in
An effort to make you fall from your position of standing tall.

Refusing to give credit when due, they don't have a clue, afraid to even look at you
Straight in the eyes; intimidated by what they perceive you can do.

Even when minding your own, they're upset because you're not a clone
Of their ideal teammate; see, you're like none they've ever known.

Stuck in a revolving door, complete with an extremely thick glass ceiling, but no floor.
Every day it is the same thing, no end in sight, no relief forthcoming.

Secluded even though surrounded by a few, what in the world can I do
To end this strain that has me stuck here like glue?

Now you spell like I do . . .

Some Things Never Change

Life, liberty, and the pursuit of happiness
Seem to be not much more than a cruel joke.
How can a man have liberty when he is constantly
Being judged because his skin has the hint of a tint?
Can that be the life we were promised by right
When we gained independence in 1776?

Everything I do must be so much better, you see.
Why do I have to earn twice as much to be accepted
In a suburb with other men that bleed just like me?
Oh, that's right, my face isn't the same hue
So I am the sore thumb in the community of a few.

Some people say that things are getting better,
Well, they sure could have fooled me.
I still feel the cold glances and see the clutched purses,
And experience the hatred in the streets.
How can they tell me things are all right
When I can't even walk on "their" streets at night?

The more things change, the more they stay the same…

My Life, My Death

I wonder what would happen if I died,
What if it were time for me to take that final ride?
Just how many people would actually care?
Will memories of me soon become rare?

How many lives did I really touch?
To whom did my life really mean much?
What will people remember most about me?
Were my faults all that they could see?

I wonder if I will be remembered as a saint,
Or will what I've done soon become faint?
Did I do all I could while I was here?
Or did I waste my time and live in fear?

Maybe then I could find out what is true,
Discover the secrets that only you knew.
Did you really love me as you used to say?
Or to you was I just some little game to play?

An Endless Journey

As I walk through my own valleys of shadows and death,
I look to the heavens to summon all the energy that I may have left.
The plight against me in this world by the all of the powers that be,
Has boiled over to the point where there is a lack of trust and chemistry.

Sticking out like a great white shark in a six-foot-deep pond,
Recent events have spoiled what was thought to be a shared bond.
Thrown under the bus this time just as before,
Just can't trust anyone as far as you can throw them across the floor.

All I have to do is take a look around and see,
Being in this so-called corporate world is not all it's cracked up to be.
The same barriers that held us back in many of the years past,
Have shown themselves as a new ceiling made of glass.

I know that the Lord has promised to deliver me from all of this,
And in the meantime I just have to stay strong while I'm in the midst
Of all the drama from people who I will not even miss,
When I depart and remove them from my list of my associates.

Maintaining composure seems to be the name of the game,
Though sometimes I want to lose it when I get the blame
For someone else's misdeeds and mistakes that lead to strife,
Is it really a good thing to be climbing this corporate ladder for life?

Is This the End?

Here I sit, right by someone but still alone,
Like an outcast, an orphan without a home.
How I long for the old days, the way it used to be,
I still hear "I love you," but no longer feel it on me.

I wonder what happened, what did I do wrong?
The last time I felt a touch, it seems to be so long.
Will we get it right, because my broken heart needs to mend?
I don't know what will happen, but does this look like the end?

Which Way is the Truth?

Does she really love me,
Or is that just what she speaks?
I try to be all that I can be
But something in our relationship still leaks.

Sometimes I can't seem to comprehend,
A number of the things she does.
She makes me think that it's the end,
Then it goes back to how it was.

Which one of these is real,
And which one of them is a fake?
How do I know what she feels?
Which side of her should I take?

I love her with all my heart,
And she says that she loves me,
Must I continue to be pierced with this dart
Of mass confusion as far as the eye can see?

The Closet

Give up?

No, I guess I should not,
But why do I feel my drive is in vain?
Every time I step forward, I get pushed back,
I get off track and under attack; it's hard to handle that.

Yet I still try, but I don't know why,
I guess my emotions override my good sense.
Why should I hurt? Do I deserve it?
Maybe the errors of my past have caused all this.

Maybe my feelings moved too fast and are too strong,
But I thought you felt the same all along.
I don't even hear from you; no calls, no letters,
Perhaps I am the problem, you probably deserve better.

So I'm asking you, what is it you want?
You seem to be so unclear when it comes to this.
I no longer know what to think, I wish I didn't have to guess
But rather know; to release me from my closet of confusion,
The fact it, you have to fill in the rest . . .

Death of Desire

What happens when a dream dies?
It leaves you feeling empty and with tears in your eyes.
Even from within your lonely heart cries,
And makes you want to shrink back and sever all your ties.

What happen when you lose a dream?
The pain builds inside you until it makes you scream.
It clumps up in your soul like curdled cream,
It rips away your desire, or at least that's how it seems.

A dream I once had is now gone,
It left me perplexed and so alone.
I felt like a dog that had just lost his bone,
I isolated myself into my own little zone.

Maybe one day I can relive my vision,
Maybe right now I'm just going through transition.
Maybe then my heart and reality will move with precision,
And just maybe that dream will finally come to the same decision.

Hank Gathers

Words about a man whose immense basketball prowess went from being celebrated to being categorized as unrealized potential in just one brief moment on the court

As I watched the
Ball go through
The rim
People yelled from
The left and the
Right
Good job they
Said as I held
My hands up high
And then at once
I fell
And I died.

Absentee Fathers

May I ask, "Where are they now?"
Why are they not there to show the family how?
Why is it that they won't step up to the plate?
Don't they know that's what makes kids grow up to hate?

It's a shame what some kids go through,
No one to give them a ball and no one to show them what to do.
Father-child events don't exist with only just one,
Having the other one there is second to none.

To the men, please don't sell your kids out,
Be there to show them what this life is really all about.
Don't look at it as a chore; it should not be a bother,
Any male can be a dad, but it takes a real man to be a father.

Please Forgive Me

I need you to forgive me,
For I have not been all that I should.
From what I can plainly see,
I have not done all that I could.

There were some things I said,
That I really did not mean,
I made your heart as heavy as lead,
And I was not there for you to lean.

I have done so many things wrong,
Too numerous to begin to count,
I kept singing the same sad song,
While your pain continued to mount.

But I promise that things will change,
I am nothing like I used to be,
I can move my spirit into your range,
As long as you can just forgive me.

Love Hurts

How many times do you forgive?
Because getting hurt constantly is no way to live.
How many times do you go back?
When your love keeps sliding way off track.

You wish that it were easy to understand,
How you can let love seemingly get out of hand.
Why was your heart crushed by the one you love
When you thought you two fit together like a glove?

You get tired of crying out with tears,
But losing that love is your greatest fear.
Around every corner is another test,
The agony sometimes makes it hard to rest.

What in the world can you possibly do?
How can you make the bond of love stick like glue?
How can you make things work every single day?

All I know that you can really do is pray…

Tomorrow Is Not Promised

Where would you go right now if you died?
There will be no place to run and hide.
Will your spirit burn with no apparent end?
Or will your spirit abide with paradise as a friend?

Can you imagine streets paved with gold?
Acres of land so great it can never be told.
No more pain and no more shedding of tears,
No more dying and nothing left to fear.

Now can you imagine streets laced with fire
Where a drop of water is your only desire?
You cry out to Jesus, "Lord, please wait."
He says to you, "My child, it is too late."

You can choose today which way you will go,
Will you take heaven, a place with no snow?
What about hell, a place full of sorrow?
Better make the choice now, will you even see tomorrow?

Where Is My Help?

When everything seems to be going right,
Why are there so many things wrong?
When all looks fine within my sight,
Why do my days seem endlessly long?

When I try to do all that I do,
Why does nothing appear to work?
When I attempt to make all things new,
Why does all of the old seem to lurk?

When I give my all to help my friends,
Why is there no one there for me?
When I walk with them to the very end,
Why does "I" come well before the "we"?

When will I be able to find someone to help me?
And why does the church seem to not care?
When I walk through the doors will they be able to see
Why I feel the weight of depression on my back like a bear?

Will these things ever change?
Will I ever have a shoulder upon which to lean?
Will what I need ever come into range?
Or am I doomed to struggle to wipe my slate clean?

Help Me, Please

What is pain?

Pain comes when your heart has been torn apart
By the one you love . . .
As the thoughts of her run through your mind,
You weep as if it is the only thing that you can do,
But then again, maybe it is because nothing seems new.

Even now, in tears I write this to try to escape
My own lonely thoughts.
Is everyone around me gone?
No, but it sure feels that way today.
No one to talk to, no one to turn to, what do I do?
I feel so isolated, alone on a desert isle
Trapped in mental state where I can't be found for a while.

Do I deserve to feel this way?
What have I done to earn this pitiful state?
Who knows? Does anyone have a clue?
Maybe I am just resistant to happiness and doomed
To a lifetime of the hurt and misery that to me is due.

I have worked so hard, had heavy prices to pay,
But for what? Not for this, I hope and pray.
If it sounds like I'm asking "Why me?"
I am…
And if anyone can help me, please
Pull my heart from underneath her feet.

Help me, please…

Life's Lessons

Where are the real men out there today?
We just lost another boy in a violent way
Who was led astray by the idea of an easy pay day.
Ray is no longer with us physically because
His spirit left his body as he lay on the pavement
In a wave of gun spray…
A life lost far too quickly, hitting like a
Ton of bricks when the news got to me.
A rain cloud so thick that it made my heart sick.

What men in his life showed him that
God is the plan to have true success
In this land and led by both example and talk,
Communicating the responsibility you spoke of with your
Words, but more importantly with how you walk?

Who took his competitive fire and molded it
To help him wade through Flint's muck and mire?
Did anyone take that athletic skill and translate
It into life's lessons to live in the prosperity of God's will?
Did I do enough in the limited time we spent?
Did I owe him more than a pound and a hug when away he went?
I know this much, all real men need to step in,
Fill the void and foot the bill for the lives of these
Boys; to help them see the truth and escape all of the noise.

Life's Lessons

How can the depressing rain from the death of this young man
Not be in vain?
Only if we all learn from his life even
Through all the pain; "Rest in peace?" No,
I think not because his body is the only thing
Laying in the ground without a shot at
Impacting others now. His spirit can still help
If we carry the lessons, both good and bad,
With everything we've got and all of our know-how.

So, what are we going to do men?

Epilogue

T - Tool
I - Intended for
M - Mapping life's
E - Events

Time is the entity that governs everything in our lives. It controls what we do, how we do it, and when we get it done. Time is the essence of all of our lives and we need to learn to embrace it in order to operate effectively and efficiently. Bear in mind that God's view of time is not like ours and we really do not have the mental capacity to truly understand it. "But, beloved, be not ignorant of this one thing, that one day is with the Lord as a thousand years, and a thousand years as one day" (2 Peter 3:8).

Only His mind is infinite; therefore He has no limit to His concept of time. We need to understand how to utilize the time we have in order to maximize our potential and move forward to our destinies. There is no use trying to see the totality of time, but rather we must use the time we have in the present to set our future in motion by seeking only to do God's will. There is enough malevolence in the world we live in daily that we need to focus on conquering in Jesus' name as opposed to trying to look too far into what will be forthcoming.

"He hath made every thing beautiful in his **time**: also he hath set the world in their heart, so that no man can find out the work that God maketh from the beginning to the end" (Eccl. 3:11, emphasis added).

"But seek ye first the kingdom of God, and his righteousness; and all these things shall be added unto you. Take therefore no thought for the morrow: for the morrow shall take thought for the things of itself. Sufficient unto the day is the evil thereof" (Matt. 6:33-34).

Thank you for taking the time to read this work of my heart. I trust that there is something located in the words within that aligned directly with the portion of your life that you are going through or have gone through. It is my belief that not only will this work be there when you are in a particular season in life, but also as a reminder of the possibilities to come. That will allow readers to be more prepared for whatever comes their way throughout their existence. Remember that each season in your life is just a course of events set in their own time; each one will pass and a new one will begin immediately thereafter. Knowing this will prepare you to deal with both the good and the bad, understanding that both will be present in their appointed moments in time. Ready yourself for each situation by expanding your expectations of what is possible and always anticipate the unexpected. May God bless you as you travel through all your life's experiences.

www.ingramcontent.com/pod-product-compliance
Lightning Source LLC
Chambersburg PA
CBHW030328080526
44584CB00012B/769